Life Between Lives

A. P. Sinnett

Kessinger Publishing's Rare Reprints

Thousands of Scarce and Hard-to-Find Books on These and other Subjects!

- Americana
- Ancient Mysteries
- Animals
- Anthropology
- Architecture
- Arts
- Astrology
- Bibliographies
- Biographies & Memoirs
- Body, Mind & Spirit
- Business & Investing
- Children & Young Adult
- Collectibles
- Comparative Religions
- Crafts & Hobbies
- Earth Sciences
- Education
- Ephemera
- Fiction
- Folklore
- Geography
- Health & Diet
- History
- Hobbies & Leisure
- Humor
- Illustrated Books
- Language & Culture
- Law
- Life Sciences

- Literature
- Medicine & Pharmacy
- Metaphysical
- Music
- Mystery & Crime
- Mythology
- Natural History
- Outdoor & Nature
- Philosophy
- Poetry
- Political Science
- Science
- Psychiatry & Psychology
- Reference
- Religion & Spiritualism
- Rhetoric
- Sacred Books
- Science Fiction
- Science & Technology
- Self-Help
- Social Sciences
- Symbolism
- Theatre & Drama
- Theology
- Travel & Explorations
- War & Military
- Women
- Yoga
- *Plus Much More!*

We kindly invite you to view our catalog list at:
http://www.kessinger.net

CHAPTER IV

LIFE BETWEEN LIVES

WHEN the great experiment which culminated in the theosophical movement was set on foot, we can easily see now that was impossible to say everything all at once. Only by slow degrees the earlier students realised the stupendous magnitude of the task they had in hand when endeavouring to comprehend the true inner meaning of human life and the mysteries of nature surrounding it in all directions. Blundering misconception was inevitable, and looked at from the loftier levels did not much matter in the beginning. The question was, could current humanity be regarded as ripe for fuller teaching concerning that realm of super-physical knowledge which might, to some extent, later on be open for all who desired to enter. Again, as it happened, the idea of reincarnation and Karma became not unnaturally the subject of close attention. Spiritualists had turned their observation away from physical life, concentrating it on the conditions of consciousness following on the change called death. But the early theosophist was engaged in a different investigation; that which pointed to the ultimate consequences of physical life, fully recognised as the area in which causes of all kinds were to be engendered. Worst of all, a tendency arose amongst early theo-

sophical students of thinking, with something like
contempt, of the periods to be spent on other planes
between physical lives. From the point of view even
of spreading belief in reincarnation and the con-
tinuity of ego consciousness from one life to another,
it was an immense mistake to ignore in that way the
importance of intervening periods. A still more
ghastly mistake was made in offending the whole body
of spiritualists by misrepresentation of the intervening
period. It was true enough that early forecasts of the
theosophical revelation hinted at some mistakes concerning future super-physical life which were apt to
arise from studies dependent on commonplace human
mediumship. But the mistakes made by spiritualists
were really of a minor order compared with those of
early theosophists, who took up an attitude of hostility
to spiritualism. That movement, as I have already
explained in a former chapter, ought to have been
regarded as the highway leading to theosophical enlightenment. But now, at all events, without stopping to distribute blame among the earliest writers on
theosophical subjects, we may be content to avail ourselves of gradually expanded knowledge concerning
the enormous importance and variety of the conditions
attending life between physical plane lives. Vaguely
it was imagined at first that the Astral World, or
Concentric Sphere surrounding the physical globe,
was a comfortless region which good people were
enabled to slip through easily on their way to the more
dignified conditions of the Manasic Sphere or Plane
beyond. This habit of thought led to the treatment
in some early theosophical writings of the Astral
Plane as altogether a region of ignominy and delu-
sion, at the same time putting an entirely false com-
plexion upon existence in the Manasic realm, described

as the devachanic state and treated as the goal
to which all theosophists should aspire.   Certainly
the earliest theosophical books gave us a good deal of
sound rudimentary teaching concerning the constitution of the solar system, the downward and upward
arcs of evolution, the progress of root races and so
forth, but in all that relates to the Astral and Manasic
Planes the earliest books were hopelessly misleading.
As usual, expanded teaching opened out illimitable
vistas of enquiry, and while we are now in a position
to comprehend to some extent the nature of existence
on the various levels of the Astral World, and the
enormous importance of the periods spent there by
egos passing on from the physical life, the whole subject assumes an aspect which constitutes little less than
a revelation in itself.   Thus, in proceeding to define,
as far as I am able at present, the varied conditions
of life in the Astral World, I must not be supposed to
disparage the almost inconceivable dignity of existence on the Manasic Plane, although the kind of existence there, described in the beginning as the
devachanic state, is a condition, as will be seen
shortly, of much less importance than was at first
supposed.

The Astral World, to which everyone born to die
will pass on after leaving physical life for a time, is a
realm of stupendous magnitude, not to be thought of
as a mysterious next world independent of time and
space.   The Astral World is as definitely an envelope
of matter surrounding the physical globe as the
atmosphere itself, although so enormous in magnitude
that the atmosphere may be thought of relatively as
a mere skin on the surface of the globe.   It is difficult,
but not impossible, to use terms of measurement bor-
rowed from physical experience in dealing with the

Astral World. Although the matter of which the Astral World is composed makes no appeal to physical senses, to some extent it shares the characteristics of the atmosphere in being denser at its lower levels and thus it is difficult to determine the external boundary of the Astral World, just as it is difficult to determine the external boundary of the atmosphere. But, at all events, that boundary is to be thought of as lying beyond the surface of the earth in all directions to an extent to be measured by not merely thousands but by tens of thousands of miles, although we cannot truly say by hundreds of thousands. Anyhow, the physical globe of the earth with its 8,000 miles of diameter is a mere kernel in the middle of the real earth which includes the Astral envelope as part of itself in all respects, whether we think of it in its material aspect or in that which affects human consciousness active within it.

And the first thought to be held firmly in the mind in connection with all studies of the Astral Plane is that which enables us to feel that to every consciousness active within it, it is just as real, solid and definite a phase of nature as that with which, on the physical plane, the five physical senses make us familiar. It is difficult but necessary to embrace the thought that what in ordinary life we think of as real matter, while other varieties seem relatively less real, is itself unreal to senses of a different order. Suppose we imagine ourselves in a physical house, working with physical senses. Intellectually, we may know that we are also, when so situated, at a definite region of the Astral World, which not alone surrounds us but interpenetrates all other manifestations of matter. Suppose we are suddenly enabled to escape from imprisonment in the five senses and to exercise the corresponding senses belonging to the Astral World, at once the astral phenomena around us become as real and definite as the others were to the other senses. And the physical plane walls, floor and ceiling do not so much become pervious to the passage through them of whatever new vehicle of consciousness we find ourselves inhabiting, the walls, etc., have simply ceased to exist from the new point of view. They are no prison in which the man in his astral vehicle is confined and from which he can only escape through its molecular interstices; they offer no impediment to his movements whatever. And the phenomena of the Astral World around him have in turn become the realities, the hard, solid, definite realities belonging to his new variety of life. And now he may begin to explore the enormous region or new world he has entered, leaving utterly behind him the aspects of nature which, before, he regarded as the only realities. For entities of an ordinary or less developed type those former realities are no longer within the range of perception. Only in the case of entities somewhat more advanced will physical phenomena remain within the reach of perceptions which are analogous, though, as it were, inverted to those which sometimes enable physically embodied consciousness to cognise astral phenomena. The astral entity must be, in fact, clairvoyant from his point of view in order to be able to cognise matter in physical manifestation. Conditions favouring such cognition may be considered later. Having, as it were, transferred our imagination to the magnificent Astral Realm we are endeavouring to understand, let us try to appreciate in some measure its enormously varied aspects, and leaving the physical earth behind us, ascend in imagination to a new series of concentric envelopes which represent the seven main sub-planes, to use the conventional phrase, of the Astral World. In dealing with such phenomena it is tiresome to be always stopping to say that what we call a plane is, of course, really a part of a sphere, but that thought may always be held at the back of the mind in dealing with the sub-planes.

Now the sub-planes are really as varied in their material aspects as the conditions of consciousness within them. If we begin to deal very broadly with their main characteristics, beginning with No. 1 as the lowest, the actual locality to be thought of is far submerged below the surface of the physical earth, although, following on what I have already endeavoured to indicate, the solid rock of the earth's interior is non-existent to consciousness on those submerged levels. Or, to be more exact, only contributes to their distressful character. But sub-plane No. 1, though it would be an inconceivably horrible region to visit from the point of view of an ordinary human entity on the Astral Plane, is one with which humanity has rarely anything to do. It is normally a region of decaying elemental forms, the residuum of early elemental nature belonging to the conditions of the globe before inhabitation by the higher orders of life. The enemies of the divine programme commonly spoken of as the Black Powers, whose origin and activities may be discussed more fully later on, will sometimes endeavour to stir these objectionable elemental forms into activity, so that it has been necessary during the convulsions of the great war, for representatives of divine power to descend to that horrible region, sub-plane No. 1, there to combat the hostile schemes just referred to. Sub-plane No. 2 however, still to be thought of as regards locality in the submerged region, is indeed one with which humanity in its worst and most degraded manifestations has very definitely something to do. That, in fact, is the real hell of nature, so absurdly caricatured by conventional theology. One might here diverge into an indignant protest against the ghastly nonsense associated in mediæval thinking with the fiery torment of the infernal regions. Lurid descriptions of agonising torture in the fiery hell of mediæval imagination must have produced much mental suffering for people submissive to priestly teaching that has burdened the churches with no small volume of evil Karma; especially as the ghastly theories of hell, which, till lately have been supported by church teaching, describe its horrors as eternal in their duration. I am not going to represent the horrors of the real hell as even relatively insignificant, but the fundamental fact to be always born in mind in connection with that, is that they are distinctly curative in their purpose and never protracted beyond the period at which cures may be effected. I prefer, however, to defer the more elaborate treatment of this subject to a later opportunity. For the vast majority of offending mortals, the relatively mild purgatorial region to be described as sub-plane No. 3 is the only one on which the apprehension need be centred. Experience of No. 2 can only be due, as I have said, to human entities whose lives have been steeped in evil propensities far outweighing those commonly regarded as vicious or criminal. Again, it seems desirable to postpone minute consideration of the varied conditions associated with the detention of offenders on sub-plane No. 3 immediately surrounding the earth, so far as its actual locality is concerned, though happily quite unnoticeable, even by astral perceptions for the ordinary clairvoyant. Let us begin our examination of the Astral

World at that higher level where the fourth sub-plane is to be found, beyond which, again, nature provides for exalted conditions awaiting those entitled to enjoy them on the fifth, sixth and seventh sub-planes, to be dealt with later. The fourth, meanwhile, is a region of enormous extent, embracing so many varieties of happy condition that, in turn, we must come to realise its septenary division into what must be called sub-sub-planes, although that laborious phrase need not constantly be repeated. Nor indeed is the division between them so definitely marked as those which established a definite distinction between the main sub-planes of the vast astral region.

The first idea to be held fast in regard to the fourth sub-plane is that throughout, in spite of its highly varied character, its main characteristic is, for all who reach it, the sensation of happiness. Its varied aspects are appropriate to the mental condition of people passing on. Where happiness can only be associated with habits of thought engendered by physical life, the lower levels of No. 4 reflect physical life to an extent that has bewildered many readers of communications emanating from that relatively lower level. But first let it be clearly understood that, for the large majority of reasonably well-conducted people, whose lives are not contaminated by serious offences against the Divine programme of evolution, some level of the fourth is that on which they wake up to revived consciousness after escaping, by the change commonly called death, or in other words, from the imprisonment of flesh. Their new life is not to be thought of as a disembodied condition. The astral matter available for the formation of a new body has been clinging around them even during physical life, partly manifest as the aura apparent to clairvoyant vision. And

although the lowest levels of the fourth are in one
sense elevated in space above that purgatorial region
I have described as No. 3, those only are delayed in
No. 3 who have burdened their astral Karma with conditions rendering some stay there inevitable. For the
rest, the great majority of decently well-conducted
people, as I say, the passage through the levels of
No. 3 is instantaneous and unconscious, typified by
the familiar illustration, the passage of an arrow
through a cloud. Of course, in dealing with the conception we are now endeavouring to grapple with, we
are more or less confronted with paradox. It is perfectly true, as I have so far been endeavouring to
show, that the sub-planes of the Astral World are
localised one above another, and yet it is equally true
that they interpenetrate one another. Not to an
extreme degree; the fourth does not interpenetrate the
second or the first, and yet it is all around us here on
earth, perceptible to appropriate clairvoyant vision
and rendering possible under suitable conditions that
communication between the Astral and physical conditions of life with which the spiritualist is specially
concerned. But the interpenetration is best understood
if we think of the spectrum colours which blend one
into another so that no hard and fast line between them
is to be discerned. Though, in truth, the blending
in the case of the astral sub-planes is more complete
than that illustration would suggest. The illustration is better applicable to the partial interpenetration one into another of the interior sub-planes of the
great fourth main sub-plane. Happiness, as I have said,
permeates them all, but is to be found in the different
regions of that delightful world associated with external conditions suited to the development of any
given entity concerned. Thus, to put the matter first

in somewhat too materialistic language, and yet without that to begin with we cannot get hold of the subtle truth, the sub-planes of the fourth foreshadow in their character the characteristics of the great fifth, sixth and seventh sub-planes of the astral. So it not infrequently happens that human entities in touch by mediumship of any kind with incarnate life, and partially alive to the nomenclature of super-physical science, will tell their friends they are on the sixth sub-plane when really they are on the sixth sub-division of the fourth main sub-plane. We should none of us, however fortunately circumstanced in regard to attaining exact super-physical knowledge, be disposed to under-value communications from people on the other side, not yet enjoying the same opportunities. They have plenty to tell of deep interest, but curiously enough, during the recent great expansion amongst us here in incarnation of super-physical knowledge, advanced theosophical students are better acquainted, as regards its broad outlines, with the constitution of the Astral World than those who already inhabit some parts of it, without having participated during life in the progress of occult teaching. On the highest levels of the fourth sub-plane people have entirely dropped the habits of thought brought with them from incarnation and no longer require houses or food, even of an ethereal order; are no longer tempted to enjoy in imagination the cigars or drinks that have been sometimes spoken of from the lowest levels of the fourth as available for enjoyment there, to the deep indignation of people who cannot realise the simple truth that life hereafter is almost infinitely variegated. From the higher levels of the fourth, progress to the realms beyond is merely a question of gradual education and development.

And although characteristics of very marked distinction differentiate one from the other, among the fifth, sixth and seventh sub-planes, these are not to be thought of as involving any progress resembling promotion. An entity who has, so to speak, exhausted the possibilities of experience on, say, the fifth sub-division of the fourth, will naturally drift on eventually to the great main fifth sub-plane, the region, above all others, of intense intellectual activity. If the dominant note of consciousness of a person who has exhausted the resources of the fourth has to do, for example, with poetry or devotional feeling, the sixth sub-plane becomes his natural destination. If he has brought with him from incarnate life, as the key-note of his thinking and aspiration, the idea of guiding and controlling human affairs with lofty philanthropic purpose, he finds himself amidst contemporaries of congenial nature on the seventh sub-plane of the astral. That is the ultimate super-physical destination of those who would be described amongst us here as born rulers of men, whether specifically associated with incarnations of a royal or statesman-like type or in those which, on earth, render such people great captains of industry.

I used the phrase *ultimate* just now in speaking of conditions on the higher sub-planes of the astral, and the word may have seemed inapplicable to those already alive to the idea of realms far transcending the astral in spiritual dignity, towards which human progress is possible. But for considerable numbers, even of very highly developed people, the highest levels of astral existence constitute an ultimate, so far as the life between two physical lives has to be thought of. For, and this is an extremely important truth to realise, some very highly developed examples of the human family deliberately remain for the whole period of inter-incarnate life on the higher levels of the astral world, even though they might be qualified, had they so chosen, to ascend to realms in one sense more exalted. Their motives are perfectly intelligible and are in no way self-regarding. The principle can best be understood by considering the case of men who on earth have attained to great scientific distinction. They know, on the fifth sub-plane of the astral to which they have naturally gravitated, that science is an infinitude. But they know that, in order to serve its interests when next they return to incarnation, they must keep, as it were, in touch in regard to their further progress with the lines of thought familiar to incarnate students of science. For them to plunge into the Manasic realm altogether transcending the astral would be to lose touch with the work they have already done. They would suddenly be immersed in conceptions of nature utterly beyond the reach of mundane expression. By continuing study along familiar lines with the enormous advantages available on the higher levels of the astral, they prepare themselves for exactly similar progress when they return to earth life. Not that they expect to bring back definite recollection of new knowledge acquired, but they know quite well that that knowledge acquired on the astral would invest them in their next incarnation with the capacity of dealing with such knowledge, and thus their new discoveries in definite touch with their last will be distinctly serviceable to the progress of human enlightenment. To take a more definite example, let us think of Sir Isaac Newton who discovered, doubtless as the result of previous inter-incarnate investigation, the wide prevalence of gravitation as a law affecting physical matter. He

F

did not, in the Newton life, achieve a comprehension of the way in which it worked. He merely discovered the fact that it did work. He may now be thought of on the astral, where he has certainly remained by his own choice, as concerned with the investigation of the method in which the force of gravitation affects matter. He knows now, not merely that gravitation is a force operating on matter, he knows with scientific precision the way in which it works. And when he comes back to incarnation, we may feel reasonably sure that he will discover (as his contemporaries will regard the matter), the clue to that mystery which is still unfathomable for the science of our period—the real nature of gravitation—the manner in which it affects matter and the manner in which its operation can be suspended or reversed. Future students of science will inherit the knowledge Sir Isaac Newton is now engaged in acquiring.

On just the same principle, though it is somewhat more difficult to understand its application, we have to account for the progress accomplished as the world advances in connection with poetry, music and painting. The illustrious exponents of such arts remain, by their own choice, on the sixth sub-plane of the astral between successive incarnations. They come under the influence of those exalted representatives of the Divine Hierarchy who specialise, as it were, in the department of progress that poets and artists are concerned with. Other representatives of exalted progress, aiming at the most rapid advance that is possible towards the condition attainable in the Divine Hierarchy, may pursue another course. By the hypothesis, they will already be among the number of those who, in physical life, have made efforts to get on the path of initiation. For the moment they do not stop to think of their next physical lives. They have a purpose in view which, in one sense, is still self-regarding. They aim at attaining a place in the ranks of the Divine brotherhood, but again, by the hypothesis they are not aspiring to that result in the mere pursuit of their own individual exaltation. They know that in attaining it they will reach the condition in which they will be capable of rendering infinitely greater service to the rest of humanity than by merely bringing back to the next life the experiences of the higher astral condition. So these are the entities who pass on from the astral plane altogether to that still more exalted region, the nature of which is almost beyond the grasp of physical intelligence, the Manasic realm. I must use an oriental term in referring to it because the English language provides none to suit the emergency. Some theosophical writers in the effort, in the praiseworthy effort, to anglicise occult terminology will refer to the Manasic as the mental plane. The word is badly chosen as a description thereof because it seems to imply that the plane below, the Astral, is not a region of mentality. As I have endeavoured to show, the fifth sub-plane of the Astral is, above all things, a region of the most intense mentality, of which the physical plane can take cognisance. The Manasic begins to put those who reach it into touch with development of super-physical mentality quite beyond the grasp of incarnate understanding. There is, indeed, a variety of existence on the Manasic Plane appropriate to human entities of very modest intellectual development. That condition is the devachanic state, of which, as I have already said, such curiously misleading impressions prevailed among earlier theosophical students. Let us endeavour now to clear up all misunderstanding on that subject.

How can a Divine programme deal with people whose intellectual development has not been carried on to any important extent, but who may have been leading lives of a fairly blameless character, rich in the development of the love principle? Do not let any student of astral conditions conceive for a moment that the free astral life of the higher fourth sub-plane need fail in any way as a region in which the love principle may be exhaled. On the contrary, it is the region in which those mutually attracted by love find their companionship as real and exhilarating as it can have been during the happiest periods of their physical lives. But we have other complexities to remember. Suppose the happiness of any given entity depends entirely upon companionship of some one or two others who may not be themselves responsive to an extent which would lead them into companionship on the free astral levels. How is the continued happiness of the entity we are thinking of to be provided for? He or she is not sufficiently advanced to be able to look beyond what has really been the misdirection of attachment on the physical plane. He or she can only be perfectly happy by imagining that the misdirected love is entirely and completely returned. And nature provides for this beautiful illusion in that condition of existence on the lower levels of the Manasic Plane which is described as the devachanic state. It is an illusion, a beautiful dream, as vivid and more vivid than the consciousness of physical life. From that dream there can be no distressful awakening. It will go on and on, unchanged until the period comes at which the entity concerned has to prepare for a new incarnation. In that condition time in our sense does not exist. Perfect bliss, unpunctuated by any personal needs—for the devachanic condition has left personal needs far in the rear—will not involve any perception of duration. We can dimly understand how the infinite protraction of the most intensely blissful emotion that mutual love can give involves, as a necessity, disregard of time altogether. Such a condition of consciousness is, of course, delusive, or rather, illusive, for there is a distinction between the two ideas; and when, in earlier theosophical writings, the devachanic state was more or less accurately described, it offered for people of active mind and quick intelligence a most unattractive picture of the future life. And, of course, the devachanic condition as now properly understood, is utterly unsuited to people of active mentality, however richly that mentality may be coloured by the love principle. Advanced spiritual knowledge will in their case, even if they are to be grouped in the category of those whose love in physical life has been somewhat misdirected, enable them to rise above delusions of their physical experience.

Thus in many cases the devachanic state must be thought of as simply a blissful dream, the *dramatis personæ* of which are really no better than delightful illusions. At the same time, the delightful illusion may be coloured by a real infusion of influence from the super-physical world. To deal with a crude illustration of what I mean—suppose the devachanic entity to have been a mother, concentrating her whole love upon a son who, as a matter of fact may, without losing affection for his mother, have developed in after life a flood of new interests and affections, which, if the mother could fully understand them, would seem to detach him from herself. In her devachanic dream he would always be the son solely devoted to herself. But the real higher self of that son will, we may assume, have acquired during his life after his mother passed on, as much higher wisdom as we like to think about. He will quite consciously and successfully endeavour to pour the fruits of that higher wisdom through the phantasm of himself in his mother's devachanic dream in a way which may greatly conduce to her own ulterior spiritual development. The same idea can be variegated in a great many ways. So, though the unities, as it were, of the devachanic state are fully preserved for the person enjoying them, they may be infused with many desirable influences from the free Manasic Plane. As I have already said, those who enter in consciousness on the life of the free Manasic Plane are necessarily already, in some way or another, on the Path, and their ultimate destinies may be best considered when we deal with the Path of Initiation considered as distinct from the super-physical experiences of more ordinary people.

Now it is time to deal a little more fully with the conditions of existence on the lower levels of the Astral World, not leaving hold of the principle I have endeavoured to establish that, for the vast majority of well-conducted people, the happy levels of the Astral World (enormously more extensive than those of the purgatorial order) are exclusively those with which they will have to do. Very innocent people are so apt, in obedience to the stupid formulæ of conventional religion, to think of themselves as miserable sinners that they are only too apt, if told a good deal about the suffering attendant on existence in the lower Astral levels, to imagine themselves destined to experience these *in-propria personæ*. I confidently believe that the majority of those who may be my readers need only think of the conditions I shall describe as appertaining to life on the third sub-level as they might think with compassion of the state of those in prison as a penalty of commonplace crime; while if I venture to describe, as I shall do, the state of life in the real hell of nature, there are few indeed who are likely to peruse these pages for whom the description will have any personal importance. But no survey of after-life conditions can be scientifically complete without including a full comprehension of the consequences in that state ensuing from physical lives spent either in really sinful self-indulgence or in some deeper varieties of criminality. Let us think, to begin with, of someone who, in pursuit of his own selfish interests or pleasure, has recklessly involved others in suffering .or sorrow. Lives may be mis-spent in such a variety of ways that one can only take some one illustration to suggest others in which the circumstances may vary. Let us consider the case of a man with strong animal passions directed towards the other sex which—let us recognise in passing—would not in themselves entail any evil consequences if allowed to exhale themselves in any way that can be thought of as natural and healthy. But suppose they lead the man in question into a reckless course of—to put the matter plainly—seduction and adultery. In pursuing his own pleasure along such roads he will necessarily entail a considerable volume of suffering on other people. He may be the means of ruining young lives or breaking up happy homes. The Karma of such misconduct as that is very serious and will not be exhausted even by what I am going to describe as its immediate consequence in the after-life. It will be storing up a volume of bad Karma which must reflect itself in the environment of the next physical life. But, meanwhile, that man has got to be purified of his exaggerated habits of sexual thought before he can be qualified to enter on the purer loves of the Astral plane at large. The conditions of life in No. 3 will provide for his purgatorial purification. He will be so surrounded by illusive sexual attractions—to describe the details of which would perhaps be an offence against decorum—that the final result of it would be almost a loathing for that which used to be an attraction. It is very difficult to explain what I mean without being misunderstood. For sexual passion, however debased and carried to violent excess, may be tinctured with an emotion resembling love. Indeed, the intricacies of this subject show us passion consisting of two elements—love and mere self-regarding appetite—as entering into its conception in infinitely varying degrees. But, as I say, where its indulgence has given rise to suffering in others, and where the self-regarding element has been dominant, a period will certainly be spent by the person concerned in distressful experience on the third sub-level of the Astral : where, also, all varieties of misconduct embodying the sacrifice of others to himself will entail for the person concerned appropriate experiences on that level. Where utter selfishness has been the dominant note, and the life necessarily giving rise to suffering or discomfort on the part of others, the early experiences that follow death will be gloomy and bewildering. Slowly such a person will learn from those always on the alert to try and help sufferers so far as that may be permissible, that the only way to escape from that gloom is to learn, for the first time, that one can only benefit oneself in any true sense by so living as to benefit others in some way or another. Thus, the inhabitant of the gloomy region may be enabled at last to realise that there are others more deeply immersed in that gloom than himself, and that his own redemption can only be accomplished by the new experience, to him, of active compassion. Among the multitude of books that have been written under dictation from the other side I know of none that gives a more vivid and, on the whole, trustworthy account of such a gradual redemption as above suggested than a book entitled *A Wanderer in Spirit Land*. It truly describes the after-life of a man whose life was thoroughly misspent on this plane, and it all relates to experience on No. 3, though culminating in the escape from that to happier regions on the threshold of which he feels himself in heaven, as compared with the experiences he has gone through. The book would only be misleading for those who foolishly imagine that their own trifling peccadilloes may entail similar consequences on themselves. I cannot too emphatically repeat that very few of those who are likely to judge themselves hardly are in the faintest degree in danger of "The Wanderer's" experience. And my last remark must be emphasised still further when we come to consider the frightful conditions that attend submergence in the sub-plane I have called No. 2, the real hell of nature.

Cultivated thought has long been treating with disdain the old-fashioned conventional belief in a fiery hell. We have been laughing at the notion of physical pain inflicted on disembodied beings with no mechanism of flesh and nerves with which to suffer pain. The argument leads us to the correct conclusion that the fiery hell has merely been the fruit of misdirected imagination. But, at the same time, more accurate knowledge shows us that in other vehicles of consciousness when the physical body has been discarded, conditions of suffering closely resembling pain are specifically possible. Of course, the idea of eternal duration associated with torment inflicted on beings whose iniquity has been, at all events, associated with only a few years, relatively, of misbehaviour, constituted an outrage on the theory of Divine justice; nothing less indeed than an insult to God. How it is possible that priests and clergymen, apparently gifted with intelligence, can have been guilty of persevering in this insult, is a bewildering mystery to the looker-on. In some cases even pamphlets issued under ecclesiastical authority have gloated over horrible details, and have described children, as a penalty for not going to church, as shut up in red-hot ovens and destined to endure their agony for ever and ever. The misery such ghastly publications must give rise to makes one feel as though the cat-o'-nine tails would be the only criticism appropriately due to the authors. But leaving that idea aside, the truth is that by hideously caricaturing hell, theologians have driven belief in any such region entirely out of common-place thinking. Many people imagine that somehow or another beneficent love will cure the worst criminality, and a very wholesome fear of consequences attending really great extremes of iniquity has been banished from human thinking. Now that the occult revelation enables us to understand with delightful exactitude the abundant and varied opportunities for happy life that the Astral World provides for, it is extremely important that the picture should be supplemented by equally vivid details of what that world also provides for the penalties of abominable crime—the slow methods of cure designed by nature for those whose lives on earth make their immediate translation to blissful realms above as impossible as it would be unjustifiable. So now I am about to undertake the somewhat ghastly task of actually describing (my information being gathered from those who positively know) the varied conditions of intense suffering provided for in the whole design of human evolution as necessarily as that design provides for the blissful rest between incarnate lives of those who do not mis-use their opportunities. And again, for fear of being misunderstood, let me warn off innocent readers, tormented by absurd language addressed to them in church as though they were miserable sinners, from imagining that the study of hell's conditions has any personal bearing in connection with their own future. I do not shrink from repeating that people who lead reasonably good lives pass at once to the happy conditions of the Astral World, their peccadilloes giving rise to correspondingly minor troubles in their next incarnate lives. More than this again, much that we regard correctly as definitely criminal in connection with human conduct, will simply involve a temporary stay on the purgatorial region, the third sub-plane of the Astral, counting from below upwards. And while the varied conditions of that region may, in their lightest significance, mean little more than delay in reaching loftier levels, its lower levels are quite equal to the problem involved in the appropriate treatment of even those who may have led very bad lives amongst us. Deeds much worse than robbery or fraud, forgery or even murder committed in some desperate moment of passion, can be dealt with in realms where suffering bears no comparison with the appalling horrors of the lower hell. Practically those are only the awful destiny of wretches guilty of what a very little thought will show us to be an offence at the extreme antipodes, so to speak, of the Divine nature. Positive cruelty, the deliberate infliction of acute physical suffering on other beings, associated with utter callous disregard of that suffering, or even, as in some horrible cases, with a sort of devilish pleasure in the sight of the suffering, is the kind of criminality which takes people with absolute certainty, for a time, to the lower hell. The late war unhappily has been associated with ghastly atrocities, the perpetrators of which are in most cases now as I write undergoing the penalties I will endeavour—not to describe, language would fail to do that—but to hint at as far as my information enables me to do so. And, unhappily, at present in civilised life, over and above the perpetrators of atrocities during the war, there are people who earn the terrible experiences to be hinted at, even though their nature may not altogether be untinged with impulses towards good. I am referring to those who perpetrate the worst kinds of the horrible practice known as vivisection.

Now, vivisectors are of many varieties. And some undoubtedly believe themselves guided by eagerness to serve humanity. Though their lines of research may involve the maltreatment of animals, they at all events endeavour to mitigate such maltreatment as far as possible by the honest use of anæsthetics. Then, as we go down in the scale we shall find others who pretend to rather than really use anæsthetics in order to escape the unlikely intervention of the law. And by a short cut we reach those who, without absolutely taking pleasure in inflicting torture, are utterly callous concerning it, who even find a sort of scientific pleasure in observing the way in which extreme pain is brought about by the mechanism of the nervous system. For them, indeed, the lower levels of hell are their certain destination. And, in truth, only a few of those who practice vivisection with a real, earnest desire to soften its effects as far as possible will escape the necessity of expiating their conduct in some region of the lower hell, the least horrible of which is really horrible beyond the reach of average imagination.

But now, turning aside for the moment from the consideration of the acts in life which entail a period of curative suffering in the lower hell, let me endeavour to pass on the definite information I have received in regard to its internal sub-divisions. We find the usual septenary series operating here. And the least terrible sub-division, the seventh counting from below, is sufficiently horrible. Here, where a general sense of horror pervades the scene, great crowds may be collected together. Imagine those who have habitually revelled in the cruelties of the Roman amphitheatre. They would find themselves, on awaking to the awful future consequences of their habits, the victims of the wild beasts instead of being merely spectators. Here, at the outset of these explanations, we have to try and grasp an idea which seems a little paradoxical. Even in the lower hell it is true that people are disembodied in the sense of not being any longer embodied in the complicated nervous system of physical life. The pain we may suffer in physical life cannot be exactly reproduced for them in the vehicles of consciousness they will be inhabiting. On the other hand, those vehicles of consciousness are, to their perceptions, just what physical bodies have been and their personal consciousness being the same, their apprehension of pain is just as vivid as it would be on this plane of life. So fear, which is a ghastly condition of consciousness, is ever present to the crowds assembled on the relatively higher levels of the lower hell, associated with mutual fury and hatred leading to perpetual strife and the wildest excesses of fierce excitement. I have already dealt with the mysterious fact that in subterranean regions— for physical senses filled with solid rock—the astral senses take no cognisance of the rock but simply of the astral phenomena around them. Of course, it is excessively difficult for ordinary imagination to realise this state of things, but all attempts to interpret super-physical science in any of its aspects involve the necessity of trying, in imagination, to escape from the imprisonment of the senses.

As we descend in imagination through the various sub-sections of hell, we come to some where surrounding miseries are accentuated by loneliness, and at a certain depth a condition prevails which sickens imagination as we endeavour to think of it. There the sufferer finds himself immersed in what must be described as an atmosphere of noisome insects, the sufferer being hopelessly unable to defend himself from their attack, being—to hint at the actual state of facts intelligibly—quite without protective clothing. Super-added, in each case, to the horrible condition of things I describe, or rather, vaguely suggest, we have to imagine circumstances appropriate to the peculiar variety of atrocious criminality that has led the sufferer to the ghastly realm under consideration. Again, it will be obvious that the subjective environment of each person concerned will adapt itself to his own peculiar brand of iniquity, and such brands may vary to a degree which would make any attempt to enumerate them exceedingly difficult or impossible.

In studying this ghastly subject, it is necessary to keep clearly in mind the distinction between accidental and intentional cruelty. Even when quite accidental and unintentional, carelessness in regard to pain

inflicted on others generates what we may call bad
Karma, but not necessarily the kind which entails the
terrible curative processes for which the lower hell is
designed. When cruelty is deliberate, carried on with
full knowledge of the suffering to which it gives rise,
it becomes a karmic force of terrible intensity. Even
then, there may be variations of degree to recognise.
There are horrible possibilities in depraved human
nature which have, in some cases, rendered people
capable of deriving pleasure from the sight of suffering
in others. Such cases as those are indeed difficult to
cure. And however atrocious the criminality which
carries people to the real hell of nature, let it always
be remembered that the Divine intention is curative,
however terrible in their progress the curative processes may be. During the late war, ferocious passions have sometimes been actually associated with
that which for most of us is hardly thinkable—the idea
of enjoying the infliction of pain. A ghastly case
was brought to my notice once by my higher teachers
to show how useless it is for us on the physical plane
to think of adequately punishing perpetrators of
abnormal atrocities. I need not sicken the reader by
describing what I was told had taken place in one
case where a man had, as it were, amused himself by
torturing a woman to death by the nastiest devices he
could think of. If, with a full knowledge of what he
had done, human indignation had been directed to his
punishment, nothing that could have been done to
him would have been nearly equal to the emergency.
But, naturally, a time came when he " passed on,"
and for him the transition was not to the happy regions
of the Astral World which I have been fully describing. He was swept off in full consciousness to the
awful realm to which his doings on earth had con-

demned him, where the insects already spoken of have been crawling into the defenceless body ever since. That body may not suffer pain in the way a physical body would, but the sense of horror and disgust is, for the wretch in question, as vivid as it would be if all was taking place on the physical plane. His stay in hell will not be brief. Cure in such cases can only be accomplished when the patient has somehow, with profound sincerity, been enabled to shrink with horror from the *idea* of cruelty, not only as affecting himself, but as an abstract state of consciousness. I believe there are on record cases in which, when the patient— if we may use that expression—has been of the worst order imaginable, taking delight during life in the infliction of pain on others, residence in hell has been protracted for centuries. And in reference to the particular case I referred to, I have been definitely told that the perpetrator of the atrocities in question is still enduring their consequences as I write.

Undoubtedly conditions prevailing during the late war, especially in the beginning when German authority prescribed "frightfulness," led to a most unusual rush of offenders into the dreadful territory that, in one way, we may not inaptly describe as the infernal regions. Reverting to the fate of the vivisectors, we may be the better able to understand it by fixing attention on that which, on general principles, we know to be the Divine programme of evolution. This provides for the rise of animal consciousness to higher levels by the development within it of love and respect for humanity. At a glance, therefore, it will be seen that any course of action which tends to create in the animal world horror and fear of humanity instead of love, is a ghastly infraction of the Divine programme.

But now, before we turn attention to more attractive themes, one important idea connected with the real hell must be clearly appreciated. Mediæval theology, insulting divinity by investing it with human attributes of the lower order, has treated hell as a condition of punishment pure and simple, ignoring its curative aspect altogether, and, in harmony with that blunder, has supposed the infernal regions to be under the dominance of "the devil," a being regarded as a personification of evil gloating over the torments he is enabled to inflict on his victims. One might have imagined that even the intelligence of mediæval (not to speak of modern) theologians would have enabled them to realise that any conditions which humanity can experience must be within the supreme Divine design and therefore tinctured by Divine love and compassion. Realising what I have endeavoured to show, that its purpose is distinctly curative, we see at once that hell, however terrible for those immersed in it, must be under Divine rule, under the authority, that is to say, of a being distinctly belonging to the Divine Hierarchy, and in consideration of the huge importance and difficulty of the task assigned to him, the Being must be one who certainly belongs to a very exalted level of that Divine Hierarchy. Another thought has to be taken into account in order to enable us to grasp the idea I want to convey. All work done in conformity with the Divine programme of evolution is in all cases volunteer work. No one, whether his task be trifling or important, is *compelled* to enter what may be called the service of God.

So then, we realise first that only some Being of marvellously exalted spiritual dignity, and by the hypothesis, saturated with the spirit of Divine love, is qualified to reign in hell. Far from being a region

G

dominated by a cruel and evil authority, it must be ruled by a Being who, before accepting the terrible duty, had attained conditions of Divine beatitude utterly transcending our furthest-reaching imagination. Secondly, we realise that some Being on that level had to *volunteer* for the awful work, and such a Being volunteered. No human language can adequately deal with the self-sacrifice this undertaking represents. The transient sacrifices which theology, whether in Christian or Buddhist lands, may contemplate with reverent devotion, are insignificant relatively, to the sacrifice of the Being who constrains his love-nature to direct, design and arrange for the horrible conditions of the nether hell. And the task is not undertaken for any limited period; it spreads over the whole duration of this world's life. The Being I am thinking of, known, of course, to all members of the Divine Hierarchy, and especially to those immediately concerned with the guidance of human evolution, is regarded by them, as we can well understand in view of the awful sublimity of his sacrifice, with a reverence akin to worship.

Of course, the minor purgatorial region I have described as sub-plane No. 3 falls also within his jurisdiction. And I believe that those who have passed through it and are ready for translation to happier regions may carry with them recollections which may enable them to think, when in happier environment, with something like adoration of the power they may chiefly identify with the idea of being set free.

This is the end of this publication.

Any remaining blank pages are for our book binding
requirements and are blank on purpose.

To search thousands of interesting publications like this one,
please remember to visit our website at:

http://www.kessinger.net